the guide to owning a
Beagle

Andrew Vallilla

T.F.H. Publications, Inc.
One TFH Plaza
Third and Union Avenues
Neptune City, NJ 07753

This book has been published with the intent to provide accurate and authoritative information in regard to the subject matter within. While every precaution has been taken in preparation of this book, the publisher and author assume no responsibility for errors or omissions.
Neither is any liability assumed for damages resulting from the use of the information herein.

ISBN 0-7938-1867-2

www.tfh.com

Contents

History of the Beagle

EVOLUTION OF THE BEAGLE

Man's earliest use for dogs was in hunting game for food. But even back in ancient times, help was needed in the trailing of fugitives, so the ancients developed a scenthound, which became known as the Bloodhound. In all likelihood the Bloodhound was developed through crossing the smooth-haired domestic dog of that period with the smooth Mastiff. In these two dogs, the keen scenting ability had not deteriorated, as it had done in the case of the swifter gazehounds, which relied on their eyes rather than their noses.

With passing time, man wanted a smaller dog, capable of greater speed but still possessing the scenting talents of the big Bloodhounds, to be used in trailing small game. It has been suggested that to accomplish this the Bloodhound was interbred with the gazehounds, bringing down the size and adding to the swiftness, but retaining the sensitive keenness for following the trail. From this combination is said to have come the progenitors of all the present scenthound breeds. And it seems as though this is a logical conclusion.

ANTIQUITY OF THE BEAGLE

A Beagle by any other name is still a Beagle! And although they were known by several names prior to the acceptance of the name Beagle, Beagle-type dogs have definitely been around since the days of antiquity. We find the first reference to the hounds that are of the ancestors of our Beagles having been made by noted Greeks, from whom we have learned that the small hounds were popular in Greece as long ago as 400 BC. We also have learned that this was still the case

Beagles have been around since the days of antiquity.

by the first century AD and that their presence in ancient Britain around 200 AD had also been established.

It was Xenophon, brilliant author, farmer, and sportsman, in his book *Cynegeticos*, to our English-speaking readers *Treatise on Hunting*, who around 400 BC described the presence of small hare-hunting scenthounds followed by foot.

Arrian, famed historian from the first century AD, is credited with having written: "In pursuit, these give tongue with a clanging howl, like the yelping Carians, but are more eager when they catch the scent. Sometimes, indeed, they gladden so outrageously even on a stale trail, that I have rated them for their excessive barking—alike on every scent whether it be the hare going to form or at speed."

Oppian was the third of this trio, and the one who placed the small hounds in Britain around 200 AD with these words: "...there is a certain strong breed of hunting dogs, small but worthy of sublime song, which the wild tribes of painted Britons maintain." Famed for his poetry as well as for prose, Oppian is credited with some reservation as having composed the following on the same subject:

"There is a kind of dog of mighty fame

For hunting, worthier of a fairer frame

By Painted Britons brave in war they're bred;

Are Beagles called, and in the chase they led;

Their bodies small..."

The reservations about the acceptance of the authenticity of the above have been caused by the fact that there is no actual knowledge of the name "Beagles" having been applied to the little hounds until centuries later.

Hounds of Beagle type were also known in Italy during this period, having probably come there from Greece. Some of these quite likely were taken to the British Isles during the Roman occupation. No one knows for sure whether the Romans introduced the small hounds there or merely augmented those already in that country. But it would appear, from other evidence, that all indications point to there having been packs of hounds used for hunting in England prior to and at the time of the Roman invasion.

We find reference to the hounds behind our Beagles again in the period around 1016 AD. The Forest Laws of King Canute were drawn up around this time, having been designed for protection of the king's deer. Certain dogs were prohibited from entering the forests belonging to the Crown lest they attack or otherwise harm the deer. Exceptions to the ban were "sheepdogs" and dogs too small to

Beagles are fast learners and are easily trained.

present a menace to a stag, specifically "lap dogs and small hounds." Historians believe that the latter were ancestors of our Beagles, for they were known as "Langehren," or "the long-eared," which adds evidence to the fact that regardless of the name then applicable, Beagles existed and enjoyed popularity in Great Britain during at least the Danish period.

Treatise and Discourse of the Laws of the Forest, by John Manwood, deals with the period in England from King Canute to Queen Anne. Development of the small hounds reputedly is mentioned in its study of the dogs of that era.

The French author of *Le Livre' de Chasse* was the eminently knowledgeable Count Gaston de Foix (1331—1391), whose love for and interest in the chase was profound. He describes hounds called "Rachys" and "Brachys" of the 14th century, the former generally claimed to have been Foxhounds or Harriers, the latter smaller scenthounds, apparently Beagles. These dogs had been brought to France by the Black Prince and his brother, John of Gaunt, at the time when Aquitaine and Guienne were British provinces. Thus, it is established that by the 14th century small scenthounds were known in Greece, Britain, Italy and France.

William the Conqueror brought a strain of large, predominantly white hounds to Great Britain; these dogs are said to have played their role in the development of the Beagle as we know it today. These dogs were called Talbots, practically unfamiliar to our modern fanciers, which are thought to have been forebears of the Southern Hound, which was involved in the development of the Foxhound and eventually that of the Beagle. We shall speak further of the Southern Hound. The Talbot is immortalized throughout England by the many inns that bear the name in the dog's honor and still depict the dogs on the signs outside their establishments.

Chaucer's *Canterbury Tales* mentions "small houndes" belonging to the prioress. Describing them, Chaucer wrote: "Of smalle houndes hadde she that she fedde. But sore wept she if one of them were dedde."

A contemporary of Chaucer, Edmond de Langley, author of *Mayster of Game,* refers therein to a "hare hunting" hound.

Dame Juliana Berners, the prioress of Hopwell Nunnery, in her highly esteemed *Boke of St. Albans,* written around 1487, refers not to Beagles but "Kennetts," this name having been one of the several applied to Beagles then. Her famous widely quoted listing of the dogs of her day reads:

"The names of divres manners of houndes

These ben the names of houndes:

First there is a Grehounde, a Bastard,

The name Beagle translates as "smallest of the hounds."

a mongrell, a Mastife, a Lemor, a Spanyell,

Raches, Kennetts, Terours, Butcher's houndes,

Dunghill dogges, Tryndel tayles, and Pryckered

Curres and smalle Ladyes Popees that bear away the

feas and divers small fawlie."

The word "Kennett" is translated from the French "kennet," which was used to describe a "small foot hound." It was frequently applied to dogs from the royal kennel and is found in numerous ancient records. The Rach and the Kennett were frequently hunted together, the technique of each complementing the other, the Rach having been a larger, swifter dog than the Kennett, which although smaller and slower was more methodical. It

seems logical that some interbreeding between the two must have taken place during this period, quite likely beneficially to both.

The "Kennetty" is referred to by Edward II, Duke of York, in his 15th century book on hunting, the first ever written in the English language. He defines it merely as "a small hound." *The Dictionary of Obsolete and Provincial English* likewise lists the "Kennetty" or "Kenet."

In the beloved King Arthur stories, reference is made to Beagles by their other most commonly used early title, the "Brach." Mention of such is to be found in the story of Sir Gawene (Gawain) and the Green Knight. Also from the time of King Arthur, Pwyll, Prince of Wales, owned a pack of excellent white hounds, and Wales is

Today Beagles can participate in field trials in order to demonstrate and indulge their hunting instincts. This Beagle is working a rabbit track.

still the home of many quality hounds, usually light colored.

It is in the famous *Squire of Low Degree,* written about 1475 by Walter William Skeat, philologist and writer, that Beagles finally are called Beagles for the first authenticated time in print. To quote:

"With theyr Beagles in that place

And seven score Raches at the rechase."

Some three hundred years later, Thomas Bewick's *General History of Quadrupeds* mentions the Beagle as the smallest of the English dogs used for hunting and speaks of Beagle perseverance in following the trail and of his "soft, musical tones adding to the pleasure of the chase."

The name Beagle, the one which has stayed with the breed since the late 1400s, translates as "smallest of the hounds." It comes from one of several sources, or perhaps a combination of them: the Celtic *"baeg,"* the French *"beigh"* or *"beguelle,"* and the both English and French *"begle."* The English use of the word *"begle"* has sometimes been considered derogatory, implying that smallness is less desirable than great size. Should there have been any such thought at the time, we are certain that it long since has been dispelled, for it would be difficult to find a more striking example of the truth of the saying that "good things come in small packages" than the Beagle!

There is not a more striking example of the truth of the saying "good things come in small packages" than the Beagle.

BRITISH MONARCHS AND THE BEAGLE

Members of the British Royal Family have, from earliest times, been known for their love of dogs. And it would seem that one of the most consistently popular with them through succeeding generations has been the Beagle. We know of King Canute's exemption of the small hounds from his ban on dogs in his forests and of William the Conqueror's importation to Britain of the Talbot. Now we shall speak a bit of later English rulers and their fondness for the little hounds.

The first Prince of Wales, who became Edward II, was a keen huntsman who enjoyed his hounds immensely. King Henry VIII also made much of them, and there are numerous references to the "Begles" in court

Many members of the British Royal Family have, from earliest times, been known to own Beagles.

records of his time. In his list of household regulations, instructions appeared that "dogs living outside the Court must be kept sweete, wholesome and cleane." The Privy Accounts included notations of payments for care, feeding and transportation of the King's hounds; also there were expenditures for "colars and mosulles" and for their diet, "mate," plus disbursements to Robert Shere, "Keeper of the Begles." These records also contain a notation of three shillings payment to purchase

a cart in which to transport the King's hounds from Neweline to Woodstock, seven shillings sixpence for canvas with which to cover them and additional for canvas with which to cover the cart.

Queen Elizabeth I was an ardent devotee of the Beagle. Her enthusiasm for the breed was directed particularly to the "Pocket Beagles," also known as "glove" or "singing" Beagles, for despite their diminutive size they evidently were of splendid voice. So attached was "Good Queen Bess" to these little hounds that one of the best portraits of her includes them, and in France they were for many years referred to as "Les Beagles Elisabeth." It was through the Queen's generosity in presenting some of her tiny Beagles to favored friends that these miniature hounds were introduced into France and Belgium.

King James I habitually described himself as his Beagles' "dear dadde." And evidently his favorite compliment and term of endearment to the people he especially loved was one referring to them, for to him the Queen was his "deare little Beagle" and his best friend, Robert Cecil (Earl of Salisbury), his "little Beagill." Thus it is easy to see

the affection with which this son of Mary, Queen of Scots regarded his Beagles.

King Charles II, who died in 1685, was another Beagle fancier. His frequent hunts with them at Newmarket Heath were a favorite recreation and were well known.

William III of Orange reigned until 1702, and his hunts at Wellbeck were especially famed. It is interesting that he hunted from horseback, in keeping with the custom of that time, and his pack of Beagles was renowned.

King George IV had an enviable pack of Pocket Beagles and is another monarch to have had a portrait painted

Small packs of Beagles, usually less than ten, participate in trials on hare or rabbit. This is Bedlam Beagles' five-couple pack at the Bryn Mawr Hound Show.

of himself with them. There were those who criticized his pack as being too mixed and too large, therefore possibly too fast on the trail, but King George was well pleased with them, and their admirers would seem to have outnumbered their critics.

William IV, George IV's successor, was not especially noted for his attachment to animals, but his successor, Queen Victoria, was quite possibly one of the world's most truly dedicated lovers of dogs. In researching canine breed histories, it is amazing the number of breeds that can happily claim ownership at one time by this Queen, and in almost all cases it has not only been claimed but

The first Beagle was registered with the American Kennel Club in 1885 although they are believed to have been in the US before this date.

authenticated. Queen Victoria truly loved dogs, and how many of us wish that we were in position to follow her lead in the ownership and enjoyment of any we found attractive! The Queen's dogs included a goodly share of winners, too, since she was in the habit of having them exhibited at the leading kennel club shows.

Prince Albert, Queen Victoria's consort, did much to popularize the chase among fashionable farmers and nobles of his day to the point that it became one of the leading pastimes among them. He owned an especially outstanding pack of elegant and beautiful Pocket Beagles, which were maintained in a kennel at Cumberland Lodge. These handsome little dogs were enjoyed by Queen Victoria as well as by Albert, and she was a frequent visitor at their very splendid quarters. Some ten years later Queen Victoria had a pack of her own, so her admiration for the breed, as with the majority of us who have since come to know it, was enduring.

EARLY AMERICAN BEAGLES

Although the first Beagle ever registered with the American Kennel Club was named Blunder and assigned number 3188 during the year 1885, there had been Beagles in the United States for a goodly number of years prior to that time.

There had been small hounds used for fox and hare hunting quite extensively,

Beagles are noted for their exceptional hunting and tracking abilities in the field. In addition to a fine nose, properly used voice, and hunting enthusiasm, a Beagle must be determined and independent.

especially in the Southern states, prior to the Civil War. Called Beagles, in actuality they were more of Dachshund characteristics; they surely were a very far cry from the handsome little hounds we know today. One description we have found is that Beagles of the early 1870s looked like straight-legged Dachshunds, but weaker in head. In color they were mainly white with very little in the way of markings, the latter mostly what in those days was known as "hare pied." They were, however, said to be tireless, energetic hunters, their ability in the field compensating for their lack of beauty.

Following the Civil War, hunting enthusiasts evidently began to think of improving the appearance of their hounds, for which purpose they turned to England's better known packs. Thus the groundwork started toward the American Beagle of today, the most beautiful to be found anywhere in all the world.

The American Beagle owes much to the good judgment of General Richard Rowett in having made his selections of dogs on which to found his strain of hounds. This gentleman, from Carlinville, Illinois, brought about the turning point in Beagle excellence with

No one can deny that the Beagle's charm and good looks add to his consistent appeal.

that these dogs were the model for the original Beagle standard of perfection in America, which has been so little changed through the years. This standard was written around 1887 by General Rowett, Dr. L.H. Twaddell and Mr. Norman Ellmore.

Contemporaries of General Rowett in bringing fine English Beagles to America were Mr. Charles Turner and the aforementioned Mr. Ellmore. Both imported some excellent hounds, and it was the interbreeding of these three gentlemen's hounds, particularly the noted Sam, Dolly, Rosey, and Warrior, that firmly established the Rowett strain as among the most prestigious in Beagle history. There seems to be some question as to the ownership of Warrior, and whether it was General Rowett or Mr. Turner who actually imported him. Be that as it may, Warrior's influence was considerable on the Rowett strain and on Beagles of future generations.

We point with pride to the magnificent painting of one of Warrior's best known sons and of a famous bitch appearing among our illustrations. The dog by Warrior ex General Rowatt's Rosy (by the imported Sam from J.M. Dodge's imported Dolly) is Rattler, and the bitch (by Darwin ex Millay) is Belle, both Beagles being from the kennel of J.M. Dodge at Detroit, Michigan. Rattler, by the time he had reached

his importations, and it is a pity that there seems to be no record of the exact British packs from which these purchases were selected.

The only certain facts are that General Rowett's dogs were noted and admired not only for their hunting ability but also for their conformation—they were the first truly handsome Beagles seen in America. We have found them described as a well distributed black, tan and white in coloring, cobby and heavily boned, and running so uniform in type that Beagles from this strain were immediately recognizable as such. They were far beyond anything that American hound fanciers had seen before their introduction. It is also said four years of age, had won the following:

• At Detroit in 1879, first prize and with mate two special brace awards.
• At Philadelphia in 1879, first and two special prizes.
• First prize at Boston 1879.
• First prize at St. Louis 1879.
• First prize at Rochester 1879.
• First prize at Ann Arbor 1880.

Rattler never failed to win first prize at any of the shows at which he was exhibited.

The bitch Belle also did well at the shows, having won first prize at Philadelphia in 1879, first prize at Boston in 1879, and V.H.C. at Ann Arbor in 1880. We find it interesting to note the distances these dogs traveled to be exhibited, back in those days when travel was considerably less simple than it is today. Mr. Dodge's enthusiasm for his hounds and for dog shows must have been considerable for him to have taken or sent his Beagles such distances.

Pottinger Dorsey and C. Stanley Doud, both from Maryland, took over the bulk of the Rowett Beagles following General Rowett's death. They prized the dogs highly for their hunting ability and seldom sold one; being uninterested in bench show competition, however, they chose to exhibit only infrequently.

Other owners of Rowett descendants did, however, participate in show activities, usually with striking success. Among them was Dan O'Shea from Canada, who, using an extremely advanced handling technique, piloted his Rattler III (sometimes also referred to as O'Shea's Rattler) to about 23 first prize awards and trophies. Rowett

At a cottontail trial, Beagles are run in pairs. In all working and/or competing Beagles, ability and desire to hunt are primary concerns.

Beagles also provided foundation stock for the Waldingfield Pack, which was founded around 1886.

Other especially influential Rowett hounds were Raly, Rambler, Lee, and Venus. Progeny of Lee came to New England, the greatest impact having been made by Ch. Fitz Hugh Lee and his son, Bowman. The former, especially, sired numerous winners. Both were of strong character and noted for producing splendid chest measurement and bone, but they had somewhat high-pitched voices, which characteristics they reproduced consistently. These dogs and the highly esteemed Ch. Frank Forrest had tremendous influence on New England Beagles and, through them, on others in every section of the United States and Canada.

Ch. Frank Forrest was purchased by Arthur Parry of Linden, Massachusetts, from his noted breeder, George T. Reed of Barton, Vermont. The price paid was a small one that turned out to have been a splendid investment, for Frank Forrest became America's first Beagle to achieve a dual championship, having gained titular honors both on the bench and in the field. When Forrest Kennel was dispersed, this dog is said to have brought one thousand dollars, hardly surprising when one considers both his personal achievements and the fact

Today's Beagles have the appearance and characteristics of miniature foxhounds.

that his fame had made him in demand as stud for the best bitches; he soon became the nation's leading sire of winning Beagles of his day.

A pack of Beagles from England's famous Royal Rock pack came to New England around 1880, imported by Mr. Arnold from Providence. Mr. James L. Kernochan also imported some good hounds; he bred the famous Bellman from two importations, one of which was of Royal Rock forebears. This dog seemed to inherit all the best hunting characteristics that had made Royal Rock so respected a name in British hound circles, for Bellman made an admirable record at the New England Trials at Oxford, Massachusetts in 1900, and his son, Dan D, was among the winners at the National Beagle Club Trials in 1902.

It was about 1884 that Mr. A.C. Krueger of Wrightsville, Pennsylvania, brought to America one of the magnificent little hounds from Mr. Crane's exquisite Pocket Beagles. This was Bannerman, purchased with the idea in mind of reducing the excessive size that was beginning to become apparent, at least from the American point of view. Bannerman was widely used at stud by those anxious to breed in the smaller size and lovely cobby bodies of Mr. Crane's dogs. His offspring are said to not have been as attractively marked as was preferred here, being predominately white with minimal markings.

Utility Beagles, said to have "escaped" the show ring influence, were imported from the pack of Sir Arthur Ashburnham by Captain William Assheton of Virginia. These hounds were of quite different type from the Rowett hounds, but nearly as beautiful in their way and especially proficient in the field. Blue mottled with blue and tan ticking and usually bright tan heads, they were less cobby than the Rowetts, with shorter head and square jaw, slightly less heavy bone, and shorter, harder coat. Despite their strength of head, they were noted for most sweet and truly typical hound expression. They became known as the Blue Cap Beagles. The strain was extensively developed in Canada by Mr. Hiram Cardon using the foundation stock purchased by him from the original importer, Captain Assheton.

The National Beagle Club was founded in 1888. The first field trial for Beagles in the United States was held at Hyannis, Massachusetts, on November 4, 1890, with an entry of 18. Three years later the New England Beagle Club became the second to hold a field trial here, which it did at Oxford, Massachusetts, in 1893.

Description of the Beagle

Everyone knows that the Beagle is a good rabbit dog, in fact the very best, working with style and enjoyment, voicing his exhilaration and excitement in the musical, deep tones for which he is famous as he follows his nose along the trail. Additionally, he is a family dog par excellence, a breed that can bring you true enjoyment under any of the

This Beagle is voicing his excitement and exhilaration in the musical, deep tones for which the breed is noted.

Beagles excel at tracking, if this aspect of the dog sport appeals to you.

circumstances for which the companionship and ownership of a dog are needed. Just ask the man, woman or child who owns one, then be prepared for a long, enthusiastic recital of the attributes of a Beagle.

The Beagle's size, combined with his hardiness, his short coat and his good appetite make him an easy dog to own. He possesses all the true "dogginess" of the larger breeds, yet will fit happily and comfortably into your apartment or house. He is amenable, good natured, loving and gentle. He is a clean dog, seldom if ever needing to be bathed or brushed. A toweling-down to dry him when he comes in on a rainy day will keep him sparkling. And he is known for his splendid appetite, which simplifies his daily care. No rushing up of special "goodies" and appetite teasers here. You will sigh with pleasure watching your Beagle's enjoyment of his rations, the only problem being to resist the temptation to overfeed, as the amount of his food must be carefully set to keep him from becoming overweight. What a relief if you ever have been faced with a poor feeder of some other breed! Should your Beagle lose interest in his food, run, don't walk, to the veterinarian, as this is a certain indication that something is seriously amiss.

The Beagle is a versatile dog. If you are the "outdoorsy" type, he will add to your pleasure by sharing your activities. But if your habits are of a more sedentary nature, you will find him equally agreeable, for he makes an admirable house dog, basking in the comforts thus provided. It is a

The Beagle is a gentle and affectionate canine companion. This loving pooch shows his appreciation with a smooch!

sensitive nose finds much to excite and please him.

Never forget that it is in the Beagle's nature to follow trails and that if you allow him to run free, there is a risk of his wandering away. No dog ever should be permitted to roam the outdoors unprotected by either fence or lead. It is the height of irresponsibility not to protect one's pets from cars and dognappers. If you do not intend to do this, you should not own a dog.

As a watchdog, the Beagle is alert, efficient and forbidding, warning intruders in his deep, throaty hound voice that there is a dog on guard. As a pet for children, the Beagle is unsurpassed, his patience almost endless and his kind nature ever apparent.

Beagles make a splendid breed for people interested in showing dogs, for here is a breed that even an amateur can learn to condition, present and handle well, with no need for the expenses of professional grooming or professional handling. For both conformation competition and for Junior Showmanship, a Beagle is easy to work with, making the showing of Beagles a rewarding family hobby. Beagles excel at obedience and tracking, if these parts of the dog show picture interest you. In fact, whatever it is you want of a dog, you will find a Beagle ready, willing and able to provide admirably.

fallacy that Beagles must be kept outdoors, that they must have access to the field, and that they must do endless daily mileage in order to keep fit. A Beagle will prosper with exactly the same exercise as any other smallish dog, and free run of your house, plus the trips outdoors that are routine to all responsible dog owners, are definitely all that is required. If you can accommodate a dog at all, you can accommodate a Beagle. And you will find his supervised exercise periods, on lead or in his fenced yard, will provide him with fun for you to share, as even under these circumstances his

Standard
for the Beagle

A breed standard is the criterion by which the appearance (and to a certain extent, the temperament as well) of any given dog is made subject to objective measurement. Basically, the standard for any breed is a definition of the perfect dog to which all specimens of the breed are

The Beagle is solid and big for his inches, with the wear-and-tear look of a hound that can last in the chase and follow his quarry to the death.

compared. Breed standards are always subject to change through review by the national breed club for each dog, so that it is always wise to keep up with developments in a breed by checking the publications of your national kennel club.

AMERICAN KENNEL CLUB STANDARD FOR THE BEAGLE

Head—The skull should be fairly long, slightly domed at occiput, with cranium broad and full. *Ears*—Ears set on moderately low, long, reaching when drawn out nearly, if not quite, to the end of the nose; fine in texture, fairly broad—with almost entire absence of erectile power—setting close to the head, with the forward edge slightly inturning to the cheek—rounded at tip. *Eyes*—Eyes large, set well apart—soft and houndlike—expression gentle and pleading; of a brown or hazel color. *Muzzle*—Muzzle of medium length—straight and square-cut—the stop moderately defined. *Jaws*—Level. Lips free from flews; nostrils large and open. **Defects**—A very flat skull, narrow across the top; excess of dome, eyes small, sharp and terrierlike, or prominent and protruding; muzzle long, snipy or cut away decidedly below the eyes, or very short. Roman-nosed, or upturned, giving a dish-face expression. Ears short, set on high or with a tendency to rise above the point of origin.

Body—*Neck and Throat*—Neck rising free and light from the shoulders strong in substance yet not loaded, of medium length. The throat clean and free from folds of skin; a slight wrinkle below the angle of the jaw, however, may be allowable. **Defects**—A thick, short, cloddy neck carried on a line with the top of the shoulders. Throat showing dewlap and folds of skin to a degree termed "throatiness."

Shoulders and Chest—Shoulders sloping—clean, muscular, not heavy or loaded—conveying the idea of freedom of action with activity and strength. Chest deep and broad, but not broad enough to interfere with the free play of the shoulders. **Defects**—Straight, upright shoulders. Chest disproportionately wide or with lack of depth.

The tail of the Beagle is set moderately high and carried gaily, but not turned forward over the back, with brush.

The eyes of the Beagle are soft and houndlike with a gentle and pleading expression.

The ears of the Beagle should be set moderately low on the skull and close to the head with the forward edge slightly inturning to the cheek.

Back, Loin and Ribs—Back short, muscular and strong. Loin broad and slightly arched, and the ribs well sprung, giving abundance of lung room. **Defects**—Very long or swayed or roached back. Flat, narrow loin, flat ribs.

Forelegs and Feet—*Forelegs*—Straight, with plenty of bone in proportion to size of the hound. Pasterns short and straight. *Feet*—Close, round and firm. Pad full and hard. **Defects**—Out at elbows. Knees knuckled over forward, or bent backward. Forelegs crooked or Dachshundlike. Feet long, open or spreading.

Hips, Thighs, Hind Legs and Feet—Hips and thighs strong and well muscled, giving abundance of propelling power. Stifles strong and well let down. Hocks firm, symmetrical and moderately bent. Feet close and firm. **Defects**—Cowhocks or straight hocks. Lack of muscle and propelling power. Open feet.

Tail—Set moderately high; carried gaily, but not turned forward over the back; with slight curve; short as compared with size of the hound; with brush. **Defects**—A long tail. Teapot curve or inclined forward from the root. Rat tail with absence of brush.

Coat—A close, hard, hound coat of medium length.

Defects—A short, thin coat, or of a soft quality.

Color—Any true hound color.

General Appearance—A miniature Foxhound, solid and big for his inches, with the wear-and-tear look of the hound that can last in the chase and follow his quarry to the death.

The Beagle's muzzle is of medium length, straight, and square cut. The lips are free from flews.

SCALE OF POINTS

Head

Skull	5	
Ears	10	
Eyes	5	
Muzzle	5	25

Body

Neck	5	
Chest and shoulders	15	
Back, loin, and ribs	15	35

Running Gear

Forelegs	10	
Hips, thighs and hind legs	10	
Feet	10	30
Coat	5	
Stern	5	10
TOTAL	. . . .	100

Varieties There shall be two varieties: Thirteen Inch—which shall be for hounds not exceeding 13 inches in height. Fifteen Inch which shall be for hounds over 13 but not exceeding 15 inches in height.

DISQUALIFICATION

Any hound measuring more than 15 inches shall be disqualified.

PACKS OF BEAGLES

SCALE OF POINTS FOR JUDGING

Hounds—General levelness of pack	. . . . .40%
Individual merit of hounds	. . . .30%
	70%
Manners	. . . . .20%
Appointments	. . . . .10%
TOTAL	. . . . .100%

Levelness of pack—The first thing in a pack to be considered is that they present a unified appearance. The hounds must be as near to the same height, weight, conformation and color as possible.

Individual Merit of the Hounds—Is the individual bench-show quality of the hounds. A very level and sporty pack can be gotten together and not a single hound be a good Beagle. This is to be avoided.

Manners—The hounds must all work gaily and cheerfully, with flags up— obeying all commands cheerfully. They should be broken to heel up, kennel up, follow promptly and stand. Cringing, sulking, lying down to be avoided. Also, a pack must not work as though in terror of master and whips. In Beagle packs it is recommended that the whip be used as little as possible.

Appointments—Master and whips should be dressed alike, the master or huntsman to carry horn the whips and master to carry light thong whips. One whip should carry extra couplings on shoulder strap.

RECOMMENDATIONS FOR SHOW LIVERY

Black velvet cap, white stock, green coat, white breeches or knicker-bockers, green or blackstockings, white spats, black or dark brown shoes. Vest and gloves optional. Ladies should turn out exactly the same except for a white skirt instead of white breeches.

Approved September 10, 1957

Your New Beagle Puppy

SELECTION

When you do pick out a Beagle puppy as a pet, don't be hasty; the longer you study puppies, the better you will understand them. Make it

Although it allows for good photo opportunities, bringing puppies home during the holidays is not a good idea as it is usually a very hectic time of year.

your transcendent concern to select only one that radiates good health and spirit and is lively on his feet, whose eyes are bright, whose coat shines, and who comes forward eagerly to make and to cultivate your acquaintance. Don't fall for any shy little darling that wants to retreat to his bed or his box, or plays coy behind other puppies or people, or hides his head under your arm or jacket appealing to your protective instinct. Pick the Beagle puppy who forthrightly picks you! The feeling of attraction should be mutual!

DOCUMENTS

Now, a little paper work is in order. When you purchase a purebred Beagle puppy, you should receive a transfer of ownership, registration material, and other "papers" (a list of the immunization shots, if any, the

Choose a Beagle puppy that exhibits bright eyes and a shiny coat and that radiates good health.

Beagle puppies are adorable and irresistible, making it difficult to choose just one!

puppy may have been given; a note on whether or not the puppy has been wormed; a diet and feeding schedule to which the puppy is accustomed) and you are welcomed as a fellow owner to a long, pleasant association with a most lovable pet, and more (news)paper work.

GENERAL PREPARATION

You have chosen to own a particular Beagle puppy. You have chosen it very carefully over all other breeds and all other puppies. So before you ever get that Beagle puppy home, you will have prepared for its arrival by reading everything you can get your hands on having to do with the management of Beagles and puppies. True, you will run into many conflicting opinions, but at least you will not be starting "blind." Read, study, digest. Talk over your plans with your veterinarian, other "Beagle

people," and the seller of your Beagle puppy.

When you get your Beagle puppy, you will find that your reading and study are far from finished. You've just scratched the surface in your plan to provide the greatest possible comfort and health for your Beagle; and, by the same token, you do want to assure yourself of the greatest possible enjoyment of this wonderful creature. You must be ready for this puppy mentally as well as in the physical requirements.

TRANSPORTATION

If you take the puppy home by car, protect him from drafts, particularly in cold weather. Wrapped in a towel and carried in the arms or lap of a passenger, the Beagle puppy will usually make the trip without mishap. If the pup starts to drool and to squirm, stop the car for a few minutes. Have newspapers handy in case of car-sickness. A covered carton lined with newspapers provides protection for puppy and car, if you are driving alone. Avoid excitement and unnecessary handling of the puppy on arrival. A Beagle puppy is a very small "package" to be making a complete change of surroundings and company, and he needs frequent rest and refreshment to renew his vitality.

THE FIRST DAY AND NIGHT

When your Beagle puppy arrives in your home, put him down on the floor and don't pick him up again, except when it is absolutely necessary. He is a dog, a real dog, and must not be lugged around like a rag doll. Handle him as little as possible, and permit no one to pick him up and baby him. To repeat, put your Beagle puppy on the floor or the ground and let him stay there except when it may be necessary to do otherwise.

Quite possibly your Beagle puppy will be afraid for a while in his new surroundings, without his mother and littermates. Comfort him and reassure him, but don't console him. Don't give him the "oh-you-poor-itsy-bitsy-puppy" treatment. Be calm, friendly, and reassuring. Encourage him to walk around and sniff over his new home. If it's dark, put on the lights. Let him roam for a few minutes while you and everyone else concerned sit quietly or go about your routine business. Let the puppy come back to you.

Playmates may cause an immediate problem if the new Beagle puppy is to be greeted by children or other pets. If not, you can skip this subject. The natural affinity between puppies and children calls for some supervision until a live-and-let-live relationship is established. This applies particularly to a Christmas puppy, when there is more excitement than usual and more chance for a puppy to swallow something upsetting. It is a better plan to welcome the puppy several days before or after the holiday

An adorable tri-color pup. In Beagles, true coloration usually emerges around three weeks of age.

In the beginning stages of housetraining, put papers on the floor for your puppy to puddle on.

week. Like a baby, your Beagle puppy needs much rest and should not be over-handled. Once a child realizes that a puppy has "feelings" similar to his own, and can readily be hurt or injured, the opportunities for play and responsibilities provide exercise and training for both.

For his first night with you, he should be put where he is to sleep every night—say in the kitchen, since its floor can usually be easily cleaned. Let him explore the kitchen to his heart's content; close doors to confine him there. Prepare his food and feed him lightly the first night.

Give him a pan with some water in it—not a lot, since most puppies will try to drink the whole pan dry. Give him an old coat or shirt to lie on. Since a coat or shirt will be strong in human scent, he will pick it out to lie on, thus furthering his feeling of security in the room where he has just been fed.

HOUSETRAINING HELPS

Now, sooner or later—mostly sooner—your new Beagle puppy is going to "puddle" on the floor. First take a newspaper and lay it on the puddle until the urine is soaked up onto the paper. Save this paper. Now take a cloth with soap and water, wipe up the floor and dry it well. Then take the wet paper and place it on a fairly large square of newspapers in a convenient corner. When cleaning up, always keep a piece of wet paper on top of the others. Every time he wants to "squat," he will seek out this spot and use the papers. (This routine is rarely necessary for more than three days.) Now leave your Beagle puppy for the night. Quite probably he will cry and howl a bit; some are more stubborn than others on this matter. But let him stay alone for the night. This may seem harsh treatment, but it is the best procedure in the long run. Just let him cry; he will weary of it sooner or later.

Grooming Your Beagle

It is always amusing to see the joy that spreads across a prospective buyer's face when he asks a breeder, "How often do you have to bathe a Beagle?" and the breeder replies, "Practically never!" If your Beagle is a house pet and a "mudder" and sleeps with the children, you may wish to get him in a bath tub once in a while for the sake of clean white

A daily brushing with a short-bristle brush or a hound glove will keep your Beagle puppy's coat looking shiny and healthy.

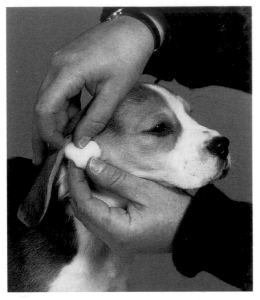

You can clean your Beagle's ears by wiping them gently with a cotton ball dipped in hydrogen peroxide.

sheets, but otherwise even the show dog gets bathed only under certain specific circumstances.

Tub baths with shampoos have a tendency to soften the Beagle coat, which is not desirable for the show ring. Show-wise owners prefer the dry or commercial shampoos if it is necessary to clean their dogs. These commercial shampoos can be purchased at pet shops or dog-supply houses. On the Thursday before the weekend show, a dry shampoo is spread all over the dog, rubbed into the coat, and then the dog is wiped with a towel. This is usually sufficient to get the dog clean and smelling beautifully without his ever having to be submerged in water.

GROOMING FOR THE SHOW RING

Every judge should be presented with a clean and well-groomed entry. It can be the difference between winning and losing! Grooming your dog for the show ring is both a courtesy and a necessity if you expect to win. In Europe this is not always the case, since the fanciers abroad put more emphasis on showing dogs in their natural state. But in America it is a different story.

Many hours of grooming represent pride of ownership and contribute to the dog's appearance and good health.

While the dry shampoo is sufficient for a Beagle in the way of a bath, there are certain other grooming techniques that breeders and exhibitors employ to enhance the appearance of their dogs in the show ring.

In addition to the dry baths, furriers' combs are used to remove undercoat. Also, if the dog has a lot of white on the body, French white

Start clipping your Beagle's nails when he is still a puppy so he will become used to the procedure.

chalk is used to whiten it, especially on the face. Bar or cake chalk is rubbed into the white area, and then a soft natural bristle brush is used to remove it all. While chalking is a rather common practice with many breeds that have white in their coat pattern, we must warn you that every last bit of the chalk must be removed before entering the show ring! The rules of the show provide that any judge finding any traces of chalk or powder in a coat must disqualify the dog.

The more experienced breeders use electric clippers to trim the white portion of the neck. The tan portion is trimmed with rounded scissors and then the two are blended in together with thinning shears.

We hasten to add that it takes an experienced groomer to put the electric clipper to a Beagle...not only does an amateur risk burning, cutting, or "skinning" a dog if the job isn't done properly, but if you do it badly you risk giving the dog a "hacked up" look, which certainly will not go over well with the judge. Much practice is needed on dogs that will not be shown in the near future, and then only after many hours of apprenticeship under an experienced groomer willing to teach you all the finer points!

BATHING PUPPIES

We do not recommend that you bathe puppies, unless the puppy has a strong smell that you find objectionable.

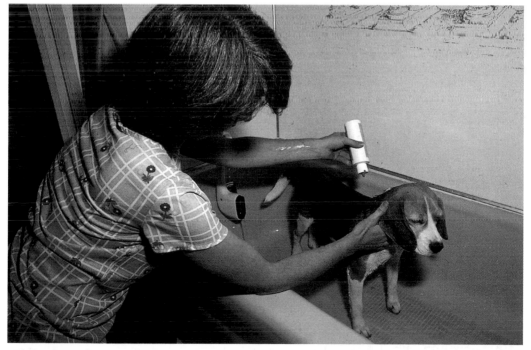

Tub baths with shampoos have a tendency to soften the Beagle coat, which is not desirable for the show ring. Owners of show dogs prefer to use dry or commercial shampoos.

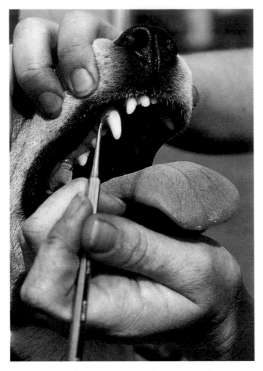

Scaling and cleaning a dog's teeth is one method of preventing tartar accumulation. Additionally, owners need to provide the dog with hard chew bones, such as Nylabone® products.

Even then, the puppy can be cleaned with one of the dry shampoos. Any of the commercial dry shampoos suitable for the grown dog will also be suitable for the puppy. Corn starch or baby powder may also be used. Sprinkle it liberally into the coat and then brush it out.

If you do this inside the house, be sure to stand the puppy or dog on newspapers in the basement or garage. After all of it is brushed out of the coat, you may wish to spray with a conditioner for added aroma. If the dry bath still doesn't eliminate the odor, and water is necessary, first try bathing just the necessary parts, such as the feet or face or hindquarters. If this still is not good enough, use lots of warm sudsy water, rinse with clean water, and towel dry immediately. Never leave a puppy to dry itself. Be sure to keep the puppy in a warm place until he is completely dry.

The puppy will probably be frightened by his first bath and will need not only warmth but also confidence and companionship with this experience. So stay with him until he is completely dry and the next bath won't be nearly so traumatic for him.

EVERYDAY GROOMING FOR A PUPPY

A soft natural bristle brush is acceptable for grooming a young puppy to get him used to the idea of grooming for a future career in the dog show world. The first few months a soft brush will actually feel good to the skin, and its use provides a wonderful intimate opportunity for you to get acquainted with your dog. Here again, a conditioner spray is acceptable and will keep the puppy smelling good. Though what could be nicer than the "natural" smell of a little puppy that is kept clean and fed well?

Feeding Your Beagle

Now let's talk about feeding your Beagle, a subject so simple that it's amazing there is so much nonsense and misunderstanding about it. Is it expensive to feed a Beagle? No, it is not! You can feed your Beagle economically and keep him in perfect shape the year round, or you can feed him expensively. He'll thrive either way, and let's see why this is true.

Most breeders soak the kibble in water before feeding it to young puppies in order to make it soft. New owners should keep up this practice for a few weeks after they bring their puppies home.

You should provide your Beagle with fresh clean water at all times except during houstraining when he should only be given water if you are able to take him outside immediately following his drinking it.

First of all, remember a Beagle is a dog. Dogs do not have a high degree of selectivity in their food, and unless you spoil them with great variety (and possibly turn them into poor, "picky" eaters) they will eat almost anything that they become accustomed to. Many dogs flatly refuse to eat nice, fresh beef. They pick around it and eat everything else. But meat—bah! Why? They aren't accustomed to it! They'd eat rabbit fast enough, but they refuse beef because they aren't used to it.

VARIETY NOT NECESSARY

A good general rule of thumb is forget all human preferences and don't give a thought to variety. Choose the right diet for your Beagle and feed it to him day after day, year after year, winter and summer. But what is the right diet?

Hundreds of thousands of dollars have been spent in canine nutrition research. The results are pretty conclusive, so you needn't go into a lot of experimenting with trials of this and that every other week. Research has proven just what your dog needs to eat and to keep healthy.

DOG FOOD

There are almost as many right diets as there are dog experts, but the basic diet most often recommended is one that consists of a dry food, either meal or kibble form. There are several of excellent quality, manufactured by reliable companies, research tested, and nationally advertised. They are inexpensive, highly satisfactory, and easily available in stores everywhere in containers of five to 50 pounds. Larger amounts cost less per pound, usually.

If you have a choice of brands, it is usually safer to choose the better known one; but even so, carefully read the analysis on the package. Do not choose any food in which the protein level is less than 25 percent, and be sure that this protein comes from both animal and vegetable sources. The good dog foods have meat meal, fish meal, liver, and such, plus protein from alfalfa and soy beans, as well as some dried-milk

Feed your Beagle the type of food that is formulated especially for his age.

While your puppy is still young, you should establish a feeding schedule for him. This pup knows exactly when his dinner will be arriving.

product. Note the vitamin content carefully. See that they are all there in good proportions; and be especially certain that the food contains properly high levels of vitamins A and D, two of the most perishable and important ones. Note the B-complex level, but don't worry about carbohydrate and mineral levels. These substances are plentiful and cheap and not likely to be lacking in a good brand.

The advice given for how to choose a dry food also applies to moist or canned types of dog foods, if you decide to feed one of these.

Having chosen a really good food, feed it to your Beagle as the manufacturer directs. And once you've started, stick to it. Never change if you can possibly help it. A switch from one meal or kibble-type food can usually be made without too much upset; however, a change will almost invariably give you (and your Beagle) some trouble.

When Supplements Are Needed

Now what about supplements of various kinds, mineral and vitamin, or the various oils? They are all okay to add to your Beagle's food. However, if you are feeding your Beagle a correct diet, and this is easy to do, no supplements are necessary unless your Beagle has been improperly fed, has been sick, or is having puppies. Vitamins and minerals are naturally present in all the foods; and to ensure against any loss through processing, they are added in concentrated form to the dog food you use. Except on the advice of your veterinarian, added amounts of vitamins can prove harmful to your Beagle! The same risk goes with minerals.

FEEDING SCHEDULE

When and how much food to give your Beagle? As to when (except in the instance of puppies), suit yourself. You may feed two meals per day or the same amount in one single feeding, either morning or night. As to how to prepare the food and how much to give, it is generally best to follow the directions on the food package. Your own Beagle may want a little more or a little less.

Fresh, cool water should always be available to your Beagle. This is important to good health throughout his lifetime.

ALL BEAGLES NEED TO CHEW

Puppies and young Beagles need something with resistance to chew on while their teeth and jaws are

The Dental Chew® by Nylabone® has raised dental tips, which are small bumps evenly placed on the device that help fight plaque from any angle at which the dog grabs the bone.

developing—for cutting the puppy teeth, to induce growth of the permanent teeth under the puppy teeth, to assist in getting rid of the puppy teeth at the proper time, to help the permanent teeth through the gums, to ensure normal jaw development, and to settle the permanent teeth solidly in the jaws.

The adult Beagle's desire to chew stems from the instinct for tooth cleaning, gum massage, and jaw exercise—plus the need for an outlet for periodic doggie tensions.

This is why dogs, especially puppies and young dogs, will often destroy property worth hundreds of dollars when their chewing instinct is not diverted from their owner's

Provide safe chew toys for your Beagle, such as those made by Nylabone®.

possessions. And this is why you should provide your Beagle with something to chew—something that has the necessary functional qualities, is desirable from the Beagle's viewpoint, and is safe for him.

It is very important that your Beagle not be permitted to chew on anything he can break or on any indigestible thing from which he can bite sizable chunks. Sharp pieces, such as from a bone which can be broken by a dog, may pierce the intestinal wall and kill. Indigestible things that can be bitten off in chunks, such as from shoes or rubber or plastic toys, may cause an intestinal stoppage (if not

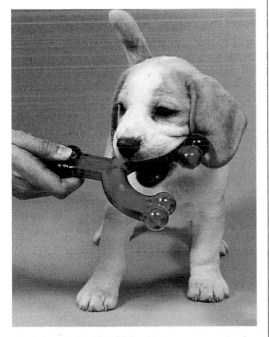

Nylabone® Flexibles® are good for puppies because of their softer composition. They come in a variety of colors and shapes, and Beagles love to chew on them.

Provide fresh, clean water for your Beagle especially if he is left outside in warm weather.

regurgitated) and bring painful death, unless surgery is promptly performed.

Strong natural bones, such as 4- to 8-inch lengths of round shin bone from mature beef—either the kind you can get from a butcher or one of the variety available commercially in pet stores—may serve your Beagle's teething needs if his mouth is large enough to handle them effectively. You may be tempted to give your Beagle puppy a smaller bone and he may not be able to break it when you do, but puppies grow rapidly and the power of their jaws constantly increases until maturity. This means that a growing Beagle may break one of the smaller bones at any time, swallow the pieces, and die painfully before you realize what is wrong.

All hard natural bones are very abrasive. If your Beagle is an avid chewer, natural bones may wear away his teeth prematurely; hence, they then should be taken away from your dog when the teething purposes have been served. The badly worn, and usually painful, teeth of many mature dogs can be traced to excessive chewing on natural bones.

Contrary to popular belief, knuckle bones that can be chewed up and swallowed by your Beagle provide little, if any, usable calcium or other nutriment. They do, however, disturb the digestion of most dogs and cause them to vomit the nourishing food they need.

Dried rawhide products of various types, shapes, sizes, and prices are available on the market and have become quite popular. However, they don't serve the primary chewing functions very well; they are a bit messy when wet from mouthing, and most Beagles chew them up rather rapidly—but they have been considered safe for dogs until recently. Now, more and more incidents of death, and near death, by strangulation have been reported to be the results of partially swallowed chunks of rawhide swelling in the throat. More recently, some veterinarians have been attributing cases of acute constipation to large pieces of incompletely digested rawhide in the intestine.

A new product, molded rawhide, is very safe. During the process, the rawhide is melted and then injection molded into the familiar dog shape. It is very hard and is eagerly accepted by Beagles. The melting process also sterilizes the rawhide. Don't confuse this with pressed rawhide, which is nothing more than small strips of rawhide squeezed together.

The nylon bones, especially those with natural meat and bone fractions added, are probably the most complete, safe, and economical answer to the chewing need. Dogs cannot break them or bite off sizable chunks; hence, they are completely safe—and being longer lasting than other things offered for the purpose, they are economical.

Hard chewing raises little bristle-like projections on the surface of the nylon bones—to provide effective interim tooth cleaning and vigorous gum massage, much in the same way your toothbrush does it for you. The little projections are raked off and swallowed in the form of thin shavings, but the chemistry of the nylon is such that they break down in the stomach fluids and pass through without effect.

The toughness of the nylon provides the strong chewing resistance needed for important jaw exercise and effectively aids teething functions, but there is no tooth wear because nylon is non-abrasive. Being inert, nylon does not support the

Beagles love the company of other dogs, especially other Beagles. Meals are more enjoyable in groups.

The Nylabone® Wishbone® is a fun chew toy for your Beagle.

growth of microorganisms; and it can be washed in soap and water or it can be sterilized by boiling or in an autoclave.

Nylabone® is highly recommended by veterinarians as a safe, healthy nylon bone that can't splinter or chip. Nylabone® is frizzled by the dog's chewing action, creating a toothbrush-like surface that cleanses the teeth and massages the gums. Nylabone®, the only chew products made of flavor-impregnated solid nylon, are available in your local pet shop. Nylabone® is superior to the cheaper bones because it is made of virgin nylon, which is the strongest and longest-lasting type of nylon available. The cheaper bones are made from recycled or re-ground nylon scraps, and have a tendency to break apart and split easily.

Nothing, however, substitutes for periodic professional attention for your Beagle's teeth and gums, not any more than your toothbrush can do that for you. Have your Beagle's teeth cleaned at least once a year by your veterinarian (twice a year is better) and he will be happier, healthier, and far more pleasant to live with.

Training Your Beagle

You owe proper training to your Beagle. The right and privilege of being trained is his birthright; and whether your Beagle is going to be a handsome, well-mannered housedog and companion, a show dog, or whatever possible use he may be put to, the basic training is always the same—all must start with basic obedience, or what might be called "manner training."

Your Beagle must come instantly when called and obey the "Sit" or "Down" command just as fast; he must walk quietly at "Heel," whether on or off lead. He must be mannerly and polite wherever he goes; he must be polite to strangers on the street and in stores. He must be mannerly in the presence of other dogs. He must not bark at children on roller skates, motorcycles, or other domestic animals. And he must be restrained from chasing cats. It is not a dog's inalienable right to chase cats, and he must be reprimanded for it.

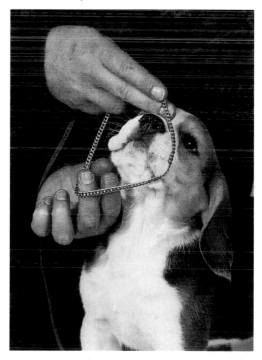

Your puppy should become used to a collar as soon as possible. If he is very young, a thin choke-chain collar can be used, but you will need a larger, heavier one for when he is older.

Jumping up on people should be discouraged. If your dog does this, gently putting your knee up into his chest should do the trick.

PROFESSIONAL TRAINING

How do you go about this training? Well, it's a very simple procedure, pretty well standardized by now. First, if you can afford the extra expense, you may send your Beagle to a professional trainer, where in 30 to 60 days he will learn how to be a "good dog." If you enlist the services of a good professional trainer, follow his advice of when to come to see the dog. No, he won't forget you, but too-frequent visits at the wrong time may slow down his training progress. And using a "pro" trainer means that you will have to go for some training, too, after the trainer feels your Beagle is ready to go home. You will

have to learn how your Beagle works, just what to expect of him and how to use what the dog has learned after he is home.

OBEDIENCE TRAINING CLASS

Another way to train your Beagle (many experienced Beagle people think this is the best) is to join an obedience training class right in your own community. There is such a group in nearly every community nowadays. Here you will be working with a group of people who are also just starting out. You will actually be training your own dog, since all work is done under the direction of a head trainer who will make suggestions to

Establishing control and keeping your dog's attention are two important factors in successful dog training.

Once your Beagle has mastered basic obedience training, you can teach him tricks, such as "sit up" or "beg."

This little Beagle pup eagerly awaits his owner's next command. If you make training sessions enjoyable, your dog will actually look forward to them.

you and also tell you when and how to correct your Beagle's errors. Then, too, working with such a group, your Beagle will learn to get along with other dogs. And, what is more important, he will learn to do exactly what he is told to do, no matter how much confusion there is around him or how great the temptation is to go his own way.

Write to your national kennel club for the location of a training club or class in your locality. Sign up. Go to it regularly—every session! Go early and leave late! Both you and your Beagle will benefit tremendously.

TRAIN HIM BY THE BOOK

The third way of training your Beagle is by the book. Yes, you can do it this way and do a good job of it too. But in using the book method, select a book, buy it, study it carefully; then study it some more, until the procedures are almost second nature to you. Then start your training. But stay with the book and its advice and exercises. Don't start in and then make up a few rules of your own. If you don't follow the book, you'll get into jams you can't get out of by yourself. If after a few hours of short training sessions your Beagle is still not working as he should, get back to the book for a study session, because it's your fault, not the dog's! The procedures of dog training have been so well systemized that it must be your fault, since literally thousands of fine Beagles have been trained by the book.

After your Beagle is "letter perfect" under all conditions, then, if you wish, go on to advanced training and trick work.

Your Beagle will love his obedience training, and you'll burst with pride at the finished product! Your Beagle will enjoy life even more, and you'll enjoy your Beagle more. And remember— you *owe good training to your Beagle.*

Showing Your Beagle

A show Beagle is a comparatively rare thing. He is one out of several litters of puppies. He happens to be born with a degree of physical perfection that closely approximates the standard by which the breed is judged in the show ring. Such a dog should, on maturity, be able to win or approach his championship in good, fast company at the larger shows. Upon finishing his championship, he is apt to be as highly desirable as a breeding animal. As a proven stud, he will automatically command a high price for service.

Showing Beagles is a lot of fun—yes, but it is a highly competitive sport. While all the experts were once beginners, the odds are against a novice. You will be showing against experienced handlers, often people who have devoted a lifetime to breeding, picking the right ones, and then showing those dogs through to their championships. Moreover, the most perfect Beagle ever born has faults, and in your hands the faults will be far more evident than with the experienced handler who knows how to minimize his Beagle's faults. These are but a few points on the sad side of the picture.

The experienced handler, as I say, was not born knowing the ropes. He learned—and so can you! You can if you will put in the same time, study and keen observation that he did. But it will take time!

KEY TO SUCCESS

First, search for a truly fine show prospect. Take the puppy home, raise him by the book, and as carefully as you know how, give him every chance to mature into the Beagle you hoped for. My advice is to keep your dog out of big shows, even Puppy Classes, until

If you are willing to put in the same time, study, and keen observation as a professional handler, you can learn how to show your own dog.

In your evaluations, don't start looking for faults. Look for the virtues—the best qualities. How does a given Beagle shape up against the standard? Having looked for and noted the virtues, then note the faults and see what prevents a given Beagle from standing correctly or moving well. Weigh these faults against the virtues, since, ideally, every feature of the dog should contribute to the harmonious whole dog.

"RINGSIDE JUDGING"

It's a good practice to make notes on each Beagle, always holding the dog against the standard. In "ringside judging," forget your personal preference for this or that feature. What does the standard say about it? Watch carefully as the judge places the dogs in a given class. It is difficult from the ringside always to see why number one was placed over the second dog. Try to follow the judge's reasoning. Later try to talk with the judge after he is finished. Ask him questions as to why he placed certain Beagles and not others. Listen while the judge explains his placings, and, I'll say right here, any judge worthy of his license should be able to give reasons.

he is mature. Maturity in the male is roughly two years; with the female, 14 months or so. When your Beagle is approaching maturity, start out at match shows, and, with this experience for both of you, then go gunning for the big wins at the big shows.

Next step, read the standard by which the Beagle is judged. Study it until you know it by heart. Having done this, and while your puppy is at home (where he should be) growing into a normal, healthy Beagle, go to every dog show you can possibly reach. Sit at the ringside and watch Beagle judging. Keep your ears and eyes open. Do your own judging, holding each of those dogs against the standard, which you now know by heart.

When you're not at the ringside, talk with the fanciers and breeders who have Beagles. Don't be afraid to ask opinions or say that you don't know. You have a lot of listening to do, and it will help you a great deal and speed up

Beagles are exhibited in two varieties: Thirteen Inch, for hounds not exceeding 13 inches in height; and Fifteen Inch, for hounds over 13 inches but not exceeding 15 inches in height. This is the Fifteen Inch Best of Breed winner at the 1994 Westminster Kennel Club dog show, Am. and Can. Ch. Fircone Country Cousin owned by Bill and Sue Gear.

When in the show ring, it is most important that your Beagle is being shown to his best advantage. Every feature of the dog should contribute to the harmonious whole dog.

your personal progress if you are a good listener.

THE NATIONAL CLUB

You will find it worthwhile to join the national Beagle club and to subscribe to its magazine. From the national club, you will learn the location of an approved regional club near you. Now, when your young Beagle is eight to ten months old, find out the dates of match shows in your section of the country. These differ from regular shows only in that no championship points are given. These shows are especially designed to launch young dogs (and new handlers) on a show career.

ENTER MATCH SHOWS

With the ring deportment you have watched at big shows firmly in mind and practice, enter your Beagle in as many match shows as you can. When in the ring, you have two jobs. One is to see to it that your Beagle is always being seen to its best advantage. The other job is to keep your eye on the judge to see what he may want you to do next. Watch only the judge and your Beagle. Be quick and be alert; do exactly as the judge directs. Don't speak to him except to answer his questions. If he does something you don't like, don't say so. And don't irritate the judge (and everybody else) by constantly talking and fussing with your dog.

In moving about the ring, remember to keep clear of dogs beside you or in front of you. It is my advice to you not to show your Beagle in a regular point show until he is at least close to maturity and after both you and your dog have had time to perfect ring manners and poise in the match shows.

Your Beagle's Health

We know our pets, their moods and habits, and therefore we can recognize when our Beagle is experiencing an off-day. Signs of sickness can be very obvious or very subtle. As any mother can attest, diagnosing and treating an ailment require common sense, knowing when to seek home remedies and when to visit your doctor...or veterinarian, as the case may be.

Your veterinarian, we know, is your Beagle's best friend, next to you. It will pay to be choosy about your veterinarian. Talk to dog-owning friends whom you respect. Visit more than one vet before you make a lifelong choice. Trust your instincts. Find a knowledgeable, compassionate vet who knows Beagles and likes them.

Grooming for good health makes good sense. The Beagle's coat benefits from regular brushing to keep looking glossy and clean. Brushing stimulates the natural oils in the coat and also removes dead haircoat. Beagles shed seasonally, which means their undercoat (the soft downy white fur) is pushed out by the incoming new coat. A medium-strength bristle brush is all that is required to groom this handsome breed of dog.

ANAL SACS

Anal sacs, sometimes called anal glands, are located in the musculature of the anal ring, one on either side. Each empties into the rectum via a small duct. Occasionally their secretion becomes thickened and accumulates so you can readily feel these structures from the outside. If your Beagle is scooting across the floor dragging his rear quarters, or licking his rear, his anal

Your Beagle pup needs to be vaccinated regularly against such diseases as parvovirus, distemper, rabies, and Lyme disease. Check with your veterinarian to set up a vaccination schedule.

sacs may need to be expressed. Placing pressure in and up towards the anus, while holding the tail, is the general routine. Anal sac secretions are characteristically foul-smelling, and you could get squirted if not careful. Veterinarians can take care of this during regular visits and demonstrate the cleanest method.

MAJOR HEALTH ISSUES

Many Beagles are predisposed to certain congenital and inherited abnormalities, such as PRA, IVD and multiple epiphyseal dysplasia. Fortunately, hip dysplasia, a blatantly common problem in other purebred dogs, is very uncommon in the Beagle. Multiple epiphyseal dysplasia, more frequently reported in Beagles, is a condition that affects the hind leg joint and causes the dog to sway when it walks.

PRA or progressive retinal atrophy is but one of the eye disorders from which the Beagle suffers. Beagles also suffer from cataracts, retinal dysplasia and glaucoma, so screening breeding stock is required to avoid potential blindness or severely impaired vision to be passed from one generation to the next.

Grooming for good health makes good sense. Brushing stimulates the natural oils in the coat and also removes dead haircoat.

From puppyhood to adulthood, your Beagle's good health should be properly maintained.

THE GUIDE TO OWNING A BEAGLE

IVD or intervertebral disk disease occurs when a disk in the dog's spine herniates and damages the spinal column. Although the Beagle isn't the worst affected of breeds, IVD does indeed take its toll on Beagles.

Veterinarians report a variety of other cases that involve diseases which affect Beagles on a more or less regular basis, including kidney and lung disorders. Due to the great number of Beagles kept as pets, veterinarians are readily aware of these various ailments and should be able to diagnose them with little difficulty.

VACCINATIONS

For the continued health of your dog, owners must attend to vaccinations regularly. Your veterinarian can recommend a vaccination schedule appropriate for your dog, taking into consideration the factors of climate and geography. The basic vaccinations to protect your dog are: parvovirus, distemper, hepatitis, leptospirosis, adenovirus, parainfluenza, coronavirus, bordetella, tracheobronchitis (kennel cough), Lyme disease and rabies.

Parvovirus is a highly contagious, dog-specific disease, first recognized in 1978. Targeting the small intestine, parvo affects the stomach, and diarrhea and vomiting (with blood) are clinical signs. Although the dog can pass the infection to other dogs within three days of infection, the

Before you bring your puppy home, he should have received at least one set of inoculations. Ask the seller of your puppy for health papers

initial signs, which include lethargy and depression, don't display themselves until four to seven days. When affecting puppies under four weeks of age, the heart muscle is frequently attacked. When the heart is affected, the puppies exhibit difficulty in breathing and experience crying and foaming at the nose and mouth.

Distemper, related to human measles, is an airborne virus that spreads in the blood and ultimately in the nervous system and epithelial tissues. Young dogs or dogs with weak immune systems can develop encephalomyelitis (brain disease) from the distemper infection. Such dogs experience seizures, general weakness and rigidity, as well as "hardpad". Since distemper is largely incurable, prevention through vaccination is vitally important. Puppies should be vaccinated at six to eight weeks of age, with boosters at ten to 12 weeks. Older puppies (16 weeks and older) who are unvaccinated should receive no fewer than two vaccinations at three- to four-week intervals.

Hepatitis mainly affects the liver and is caused by canine adenovirus type I. Highly infectious, hepatitis often affects dogs nine to 12 months of age. Initially the virus localizes in the dog's tonsils and then disperses to the liver, kidneys and eyes. Generally speaking the dog's immune system is capable of combating this virus. Canine infectious hepatitis affects dogs whose systems cannot fight off the adenovirus. Affected dogs have fever, abdominal pains, bruising on mucous membranes and gums, and experience coma and convulsions. Prevention of hepatitis exists only through vaccination at eight to ten weeks of age and then boosters three or four weeks later, then annually.

Leptospirosis is a bacterium-related disease, often spread by rodents. The organisms that spread leptospirosis enter through the mucous membranes and spread to the internal organs via the bloodstream. It can be passed through the dog's urine. Leptospirosis does not affect young dogs as consistently as the other viruses; it is reportedly regional in distribution and somewhat dependent on the immunostatus of the dog. Fever, inappetence, vomiting, dehydration, hemorrhage, kidney and eye disease can result in moderate cases.

Bordetella, called canine cough, causes a persistent hacking cough in dogs and is very contagious. Bordetella involves a virus and a bacteria: parainfluenza is the most common virus implicated; *Bordetella bronchiseptica*, the bacterium. Bronchitis and pneumonia result in less than 20 percent of the cases, and most dogs recover from the condition within a week to four weeks. Non- prescription medicines can help relieve the hacking cough, though nothing can cure the condition before it's run its course. Vaccination cannot guarantee protection from canine cough, but it does ward off the most common virus responsible for the condition.

Lyme disease (also called borreliosis), although known for decades, was only first diagnosed in dogs in 1984. Lyme disease can affect cats, cattle, and horses, but especially people. In the U.S., the disease is transmitted by two ticks carrying the *Borrelia burgdorferi* organism: the deer tick *(Ixodes scapularis)* and the western black-legged tick *(Ixodes pacificus)*, the latter primarily affects reptiles. In Europe, *Ixodes ricinus* is responsible for spreading Lyme. The disease causes lameness, fever, joint swelling,

The Beagle is a hardy, happy breed with a life span of 12 to 15 years.

inappetence, and lethargy. Removal of ticks from the dog's coat can help reduce the chances of Lyme, though not as much as avoiding heavily wooded areas where the dog is most likely to contract ticks. A vaccination is available, though it has not been proven to protect dogs from all strains of the organism that cause the disease.

Rabies is passed to dogs and people through wildlife: in North America, principally through the skunk, fox and raccoon; the bat is not the culprit it was once thought to be. Likewise, the common image of the rabid dog foaming at the mouth with every hair on end is unlikely the truest scenario. A rabid dog exhibits difficulty eating, salivates much and has spells of paralysis and awkwardness. Before a dog reaches this final state, it may experience anxiety, personality changes, irritability and more aggressiveness than is usual. Vaccinations are strongly recommended as rabid dogs are too dangerous to manage and are commonly euthanized. Puppies are generally vaccinated at 12 weeks of age, and then annually. Although rabies is on the decline in the world community, tens of thousands of humans die each year from rabies-related incidents.

COPING WITH PARASITES

Parasites have clung to our pets for centuries. Despite our modern efforts, fleas still pester our pet's existence, and our own. All dogs itch, and fleas can make even the happiest dog a miserable, scabby mess. The loss of hair and habitual biting and chewing at themselves rank among the annoyances; the nuisances include the passing of tapeworms and the whole family's itching through the summer months. A full range of flea-control and elimination products are available at pet shops, and your veterinarian surely has recommendations. Sprays, powders, collars and dips fight fleas from the outside; drops and pills fight the good fight from inside. Discuss the possibilities with your vet. Not all products can be used in conjunction with one another, and some dogs may be more sensitive to certain applications than others. The dog's living quarters must be debugged as well as the dog itself. Heavy infestation may require multiple treatments.

Always check your dog for ticks carefully. Although fleas can be acquired almost anywhere, ticks are more likely to be picked up in heavily treed areas, pastures or other outside grounds (such as dog shows or obedience or field trials). Athletic, active, and hunting dogs are the most likely subjects, though any passing dog can be the host. Remember Lyme disease is passed by tick infestation.

As for internal parasites, worms are potentially dangerous for dogs and people. Roundworms, hookworms, whipworms, tapeworms, and heartworms comprise the blightsome party of troublemakers. Deworming puppies begins at around two to three weeks and continues until three months of age. Proper hygienic care of the environment is also important to prevent contamination with roundworm and hookworm eggs. Heartworm preventatives are recommended by most veterinarians, although there are some drawbacks to the regular introduction of poisons into our dogs' systems. These daily or monthly preparations also help regulate most other worms as well. Discuss worming procedures with your veterinarian.

Roundworms pose a great threat to dogs and people. They are found in the intestines of dogs, and can be passed to people through ingestion of feces-contaminated dirt. Roundworm infection can be prevented by not walking dogs in heavy-traffic people areas, by burning feces, and by curbing dogs in a responsible manner. (Of course, in most areas of the country, curbing dogs is the law.) Roundworms are typically passed from the bitch to the litter, and the bitch should be treated along with the puppies, even if she tested negative prior to whelping. Generally puppies are treated every two weeks until two months of age.

Hookworms, like roundworms, are also a danger to dogs and people. The hookworm parasite (known as

Itching can be a sign of fleas. A full range of flea control products are available at your local pet shop.

Ancylostoma caninum) causes cutaneous larva migrans in people. The eggs of hookworms are passed in feces and become infective in shady, sandy areas. The larvae penetrate the skin of the dog, and the dog subsequently becomes infected. When swallowed, these parasites affect the intestines, lungs, windpipe, and the whole digestive system. Infected dogs suffer from anemia and lose large amounts of blood in the places where the worms latch onto the dog's intestines, etc.

Although infrequently passed to humans, whipworms are cited as one of the most common parasites in America. These elongated worms affect the intestines of the dog, where

Your Beagle pup will love to romp and play outdoors. Be sure to check him for fleas and ticks after he has been outside.

they latch on, and cause colic upset or diarrhea. Unless identified in stools passed, whipworms are difficult to diagnose. Adult worms can be eliminated more consistently than the larvae, since whipworms exhibit unusual life cycles. Proper hygienic care of outdoor grounds is critical to the avoidance of these harmful parasites.

Tapeworms are carried by fleas, and enter the dog when the dog swallows the flea. Humans can acquire tapeworms in the same way, though we are less likely to swallow fleas than dogs are. Recent studies have shown that certain rodents and other wild animals have been infected with tapeworms, and dogs can be affected by catching and/or eating these other animals. Of course, outdoor hunting dogs and terriers are more likely to be infected in this way than are your typical house dog or non-motivated hound. Treatment for tapeworm has proven very effective, and infected dogs do not show great discomfort or symptoms. When people are infected, however, the liver can be seriously damaged. Proper cleanliness is the best bet against tapeworms.

Heartworm disease is transmitted by mosquitoes and badly affects the lungs, heart and blood vessels of dogs. The larvae of *Dirofilaria immitis* enters the dog's bloodstream when bitten by an infected mosquito. The larvae takes about six months to mature. Infected dogs suffer from weight loss, appetite loss, chronic coughing and general fatigue. Not all affected dogs show signs of illness right away, and carrier dogs may be affected for years before clinical signs appear. Treatment of heartworm disease has been effective but can be dangerous also. Prevention as always is the desirable alternative. Ivermectin is the active ingredient in most heartworm preventatives and has proven to be successful. Check with your veterinarian for the preparation best for your dog. Dogs generally begin taking the preventatives at eight months of age and continue to do so throughout the non-winter months.

Resources

National Beagle Club of America, Inc.
Secretary:
Susan Mills Stone
P.O. Box 13
Middleburg, VA 20118-0013
http://clubs.akc.org/NBC/

American Kennel Club
Headquarters:
260 Madison Avenue
New York, NY 10016
(212) 696-8200

Operations Center:
5580 Centerview Drive
Raleigh, NC 27606-3390

Customer Services:
Phone: (919) 233-9767
Fax: (919) 816-3627
www.akc.org/

The Kennel Club
1 Clarges Street
Picadilly, London WIY 8AB, England
www.the-kennel-club.org.uk

Canadian Kennel Club
89 Skyway Avenue
Suite 100
Etobicoke, Ontario, Canada
M9W 6R4
www.ckc.ca

United Kennel Club, Inc.
100 E. Kilgore Road
Kalamazoo, MI 49002-5584
(616) 343-9020
www.ukcdogs.com

Index